From Your Friends at The MAILBOX®

Solar System

Grades 1–3

INVESTIGATING SCIENCE

Project Managers:
Karen A. Brudnak, Thad H. McLaurin

Writers:
Beth A. Miller, Valerie Wood Smith, Laura Wagner

Editors:
Deborah T. Kalwat, Scott Lyons,
Jennifer Munnerlyn, Leanne Stratton, Hope H.

Art Coordinator:
Clevell Harris

Artists:
Theresa Lewis Goode, Clevell Harris, Susan Hodnett,
Donna K. Teal

Cover Artists:
Nick Greenwood and Kimberly Richard

D1314055

www.themailbox.com

©2000 by THE EDUCATION CENTER, INC.
All rights reserved.
ISBN10 #1-56234-390-4 • ISBN13 #978-156234-390-3

Manufactured in the United States
10 9 8 7 6 5

Table of Contents

About This Book

Welcome to *Investigating Science—Solar System*! This book is one of ten must-have resource books that support the National Science Education Standards and are designed to supplement and enhance your existing science curriculum. Packed with practical cross-curricular ideas and thought-provoking reproducibles, these all-new, content-specific resource books provide primary teachers with a collection of innovative and fun activities for teaching thematic science units.

Included in this book:

Investigating Science—Solar System contains six cross-curricular thematic units, each containing

- Background information for the teacher
- Easy-to-implement instructions for science experiments and projects
- Student-centered activities and reproducibles
- Literature links

Cross-curricular thematic units found in this book:

- *Planets*
- *Comets, Meteors, and Stars*
- *The Sun*
- *The Moon*
- *Earth*
- *Space Travel*

Other books in the primary Investigating Science series:

- *Investigating Science—Amphibians & Reptiles*
- *Investigating Science—Environment*
- *Investigating Science—Mammals*
- *Investigating Science—Insects*
- *Investigating Science—Energy, Light, & Sound*
- *Investigating Science—Plants*
- *Investigating Science—Weather*
- *Investigating Science—Rocks & Minerals*
- *Investigating Science—Health & Safety*

Planets

Prepare your students for a planetary exploration with this collection of creative activities.

Background for the Teacher

- A solar system consists of a sun and the planets, moons, and smaller objects like comets and meteoroids that travel around it.
- Planets are large objects that travel around the Sun. Our solar system consists of nine planets: Mercury, Venus, Earth, Mars, Jupiter, Saturn, Uranus, Neptune, and Pluto.
- Mercury, Venus, Mars, Jupiter, and Saturn can be seen without a telescope. They are very bright but don't twinkle like stars. A telescope is needed to view Uranus, Neptune, and Pluto.
- Surface features and/or atmosphere cause some planets, such as Venus, to shine more brightly than others.
- All planets move around the Sun in paths called orbits. Mercury takes 88 days to orbit the Sun, while Pluto takes 248 years.
- Planets spin, or rotate, as they revolve around the Sun.

Round and Round They Go!
(Simulation)

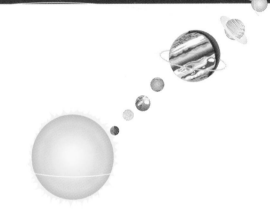

Help your students understand how planets revolve around the Sun with this outdoor simulation. Ahead of time, make nine nametags, each labeled with a different planet name. Begin the activity by explaining to your students that each planet revolves, or moves, around the Sun in a pathway called an *orbit*. Further explain that a *year* is the length of time it takes a planet to travel once around the Sun. Then tell your students that planets closer to the Sun take less time to revolve around it than do planets that are farther away. Next, take the class outside to the blacktop or another safe paved area. Using yellow chalk, draw a large circle (Sun) on the blacktop or pavement. Then draw a straight line about 26 feet long out from the Sun. Next, select nine children to act as the planets. Give each selected student a planet nametag. Starting at the edge of the Sun, have each "planet" stand on the line in order (Mercury, Venus, Earth, Mars, Jupiter, Saturn, Uranus, Neptune, Pluto). Have the remaining students observe the demonstration from one side. On your signal, have the remaining students count out loud in unison, beginning with number one. Instruct each "planet" to take one step forward (touching the heel of one foot to the toe of the other foot) for each count until she completes one rotation (returns to the chalk line). Have the class continue counting until each student has completed her rotation. Then discuss the results of the simulation by asking questions such as "Why did it take Pluto longer to finish than the other planets? Why did Mercury finish so quickly?"

Out-of-This-World Planetary Books

Me and My Place in Space by Joan Sweeney (Crown Publishers, Inc.; 1998)

The Planets by Gail Gibbons (Holiday House, Inc.; 1993)

The Planets by Cynthia Pratt Nicolson (Kids Can Press Ltd., 1998)

The Planets in Our Solar System by Franklyn M. Branley (HarperCollins Publishers, Inc.; 1998)

Stars and Planets by David H. Levy (Time Life Books, 1996)

There's No Place Like Space! All About Our Solar System by Tish Rabe (Random House, Inc.; 1999)

How Far Did You Say?
(Making a Model, Research)

Did you know that some of the planets in our solar system are over a billion miles from the Sun? Use the following interactive display to help your students get a better understanding of the order of the nine planets and their distances from the Sun. In advance, find a wall with at least 16 feet of free space in your classroom or in the hallway outside your door. Next, fashion a large Sun out of yellow construction paper (two feet wide or larger) as shown. Tape the Sun to the left-hand end of the cleared wall space. Cut out nine poster board circles, one for each planet, using the dimensions shown. Label the back of each circle with the appropriate planet name. Then divide your students into nine groups; give each group one circle pattern, three index cards, crayons, and references (including a picture reference) of its assigned planet. Instruct each group to use the picture reference as a guide in coloring its assigned planet. Next, direct the group to research its planet's distance from the Sun, as well as two interesting facts about its planet. Instruct the group to write the name of its planet and its distance on one index card and then write each fact on the two remaining index cards. Using the distance guide and a measuring tape, tape each planet in order from the Sun as shown. Then have each group read aloud to the class its planet's distance from the Sun (younger students may need help with this) and the two interesting facts. Have each group tape the three cards underneath or near its planet. Use a length of string to connect each planet to its name card. As more interesting facts are discovered during your planetary study, have students record them on index cards and add them to the display. Use the display as a culminating review at the end of your unit.

Planet Dimensions
Mercury—$3/8$"
Venus—$7/8$"
Earth—1"
Mars—$9/16$"
Jupiter—11"
Saturn—10"
Uranus—4"
Neptune—$3 3/4$"
Pluto—$1/4$"

Distance Guide
Mercury—2 inches
Venus—3 inches
Earth—4 inches
Mars—6 inches
Jupiter—1 foot 9 inches
Saturn—3 feet 2 inches
Uranus—6 feet 5 inches
Neptune—10 feet 1 inch
Pluto—13 feet 3 inches

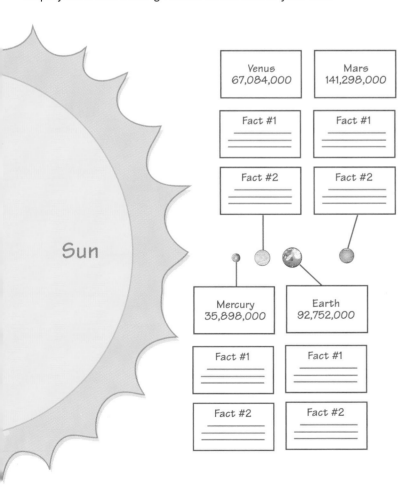

Sun

Venus
67,084,000

Mars
141,298,000

Fact #1

Fact #1

Fact #2

Fact #2

Mercury
35,898,000

Earth
92,752,000

Fact #1

Fact #1

Fact #2

Fact #2

Jupiter
482,546,000

Fact #1

Fact #2

Really Radical Rotations
(Making a Model)

Give your students a close-up look at planet rotation with these simple models. Begin by showing your students a toy top. Place the top on a table or an area where everyone can watch you spin it. Ask your students to explain what the top is doing. Guide the students in concluding that the top is spinning on the point that sticks out and touches the table. Stop the top, hold it up, and point to the end of it. Explain to your students that when something spins, it moves around a center line. Tell your students that the top's point is its center line, or *axis*. Next, inform your students that just like the top, each planet spins on an axis as it moves (revolves) around the Sun. To demonstrate this concept, have each student create his own model. Give each student one malted chocolate milk ball and one toothpick. Instruct each student to insert the toothpick through the center of the milk ball until it pokes out the opposite end. (For younger students, insert the toothpicks in advance.) Next, direct the student to hold each end of the toothpick as shown. Then instruct the student to slowly rotate the toothpick to the right. As the student spins his model, explain that most of the planets (Mercury, Earth, Mars, Jupiter, Saturn, Neptune) spin in a west to east direction like his model is spinning. Next, have each student slowly rotate his model to the left. Explain that Venus and Pluto rotate in this direction, from east to west. Next, have the student hold the toothpick horizontally and rotate the toothpick. Inform your students that Uranus is the only planet to spin on its side like this. Culminate the activity by having each student remove the toothpick from his model and eat the planet!

What a Gas!
(Demonstration)

Use the following demonstration to help your students understand why landing on a planet like Jupiter, Saturn, Uranus, or Neptune would be impossible. Begin by explaining that the planets in our solar system can be divided into two groups—*terrestrial* and *giant gas*. Tell your students that terrestrial planets (Mercury, Venus, Earth, Mars) have a solid surface, but giant gas planets (Jupiter, Saturn, Uranus, Neptune) are made up of thick gases. (Because so little is known about Pluto, it is not placed in either category.) Explain to your students that trying to land a spacecraft on a gaseous planet would be like trying to land on a cloud! Gather the materials listed and follow the steps below to demonstrate what might happen if a spacecraft tried to land on a giant gas planet.

Materials:
1 egg
1 saucer
one $1/2$" hexagonal nut

Steps:
1. Crack open the egg into the saucer, being careful not to break the yolk.
2. Tell your students that the nut represents a spacecraft, and the yolk represents a gaseous planet like Jupiter.
3. Hold the nut about four inches above the egg yolk. Ask your students what they think will happen if you drop (land) the nut (spacecraft) on the egg (planet). (The nut will sink into the yolk and disappear.)
4. Drop the nut and discuss the results with your students.

Venus—Earth's Twin?
(Research, Making Comparisons)

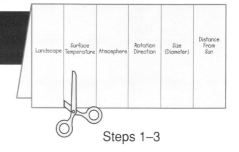

Steps 1–3

Venus is often referred to as Earth's twin, but is it really? Have your students complete the following research activity to compare Venus and Earth and determine if in fact the two planets have much in common. Divide your students into pairs. Give each pair the materials listed; then guide the students through the steps below to create an info-flap book in which to record their findings. (For younger students, make the flap books in advance.) Display each pair's completed work on a bulletin board titled "Venus—Earth's Twin?"

Materials for each pair:
one 9" x 12" sheet of light-colored construction paper
scissors
ruler
crayons
access to reference materials on Venus and Earth

Steps:
1. Have each pair fold its sheet of construction paper in half like a hot dog bun as shown.
2. Direct the pair to divide the front half of the fold into six two-inch sections.
3. Instruct the pair to cut each section into separate flaps and label each flap as shown.
4. Have the pair open all the flaps. Then have the pair draw a horizontal line through the center of the solid half and label it as shown.
5. Direct each pair to research the information for each flap and help them record the findings on the "Venus" or "Earth" info flap. (See page 48 for answer key.)

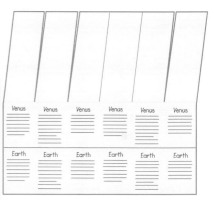

Steps 4 and 5

Wishing on a Star
(Reading, Writing, Art)

Ask your students if they have ever wished upon the first star they've seen at night. Chances are that wasn't a star but the planet Venus instead. Have a few students share their wishes with the class. Then read aloud *Twinkle, Twinkle, Little Star* by Iza Trapani (Whispering Coyote Press, Inc.; 1994), a story about a little girl's adventures after wishing on a star. After reading the story, explain that Venus shines brightly because its thick layer of clouds reflects the sunlight. Also point out to your students that if they look closely, they'll notice that Venus doesn't twinkle like a star. Tell your students that because Venus is often seen just after sunset or just before dawn, it's sometimes called the "evening star" or the "morning star." Inform your students that they couldn't live on Venus because it's too hot and its atmosphere is poisonous, but that it's a fine planet for making wishes! Culminate the activity by having each student create her own evening star to wish upon. In advance, cut out a class set of yellow construction paper circles (six inches in diameter). Give each student one circle and instruct her to write the heading shown, using a black marker. Underneath the heading, direct the student to write one wish. Then have the student cover the circle with white glue. Next, have the student sprinkle clear glitter over the glue before it dries. Repeat the process for the back of the circle. Hole-punch the tops of the circles and use lengths of string to hang them around your classroom for all to read and enjoy.

Venus
The Evening Star

I wish I had
a telescope.

Kristin

7

Pocket Planet Guides
(Making a Booklet)

What better way to help your students become experts on the planets than by having them each create a pocket planet guide? Divide your students into small groups. Give each student a copy of the booklet cover pattern at the bottom of this page and one copy each of pages 9 through 11. Supply each group with the materials listed; then guide each student through the steps below to create her own pocket planet guide. Encourage the members of each group to work together in researching and sharing the missing facts for each planet. Have students take their completed pocket planet guides home to share with their families.

Materials for each group: crayons, scissors, stapler, reference materials on planets

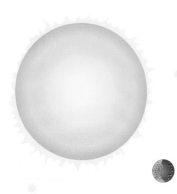
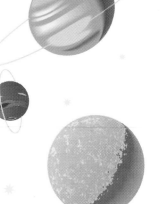

Steps:
1. Color each planet as directed.
2. Research each planet to find the missing answers to the facts. Write the answers in the appropriate blanks.
3. Cut out each booklet page.
4. Stack the pages in order with the cover on top.
5. Staple the booklet together along the left-hand side.
6. Color the cover.

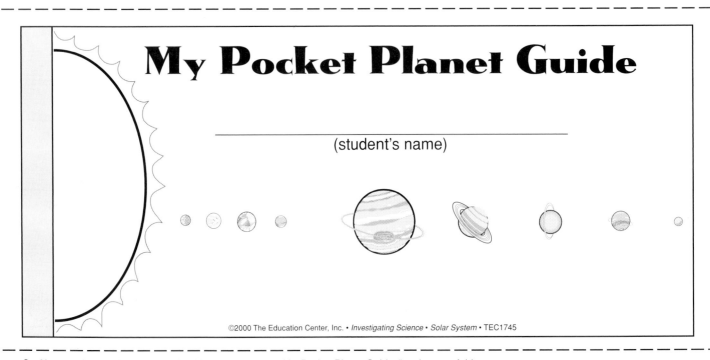

My Pocket Planet Guide

_____
(student's name)

Note to the teacher: Use the booklet cover pattern with "Pocket Planet Guides" at the top of this page.

Mercury
Color: yellowish brown

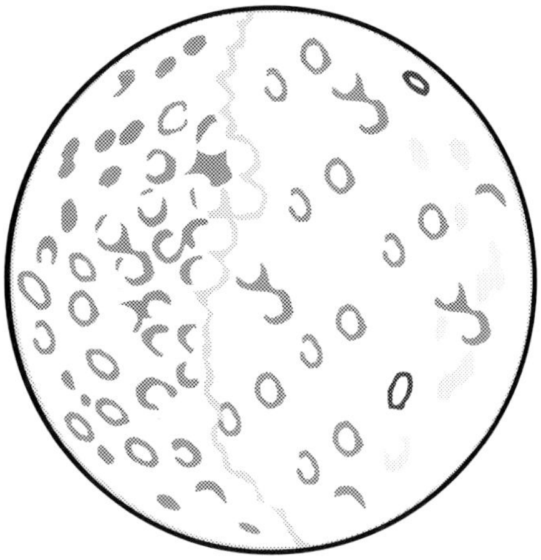

Distance from the Sun = _____

Number of moons = _____

Order of planet from the Sun = _____

1 year on Mercury = _____ Earth days

1 day on Mercury = this many Earth days/ hours _____

Interesting fact: _____

_____ ①

Venus
Color: yellowish brown

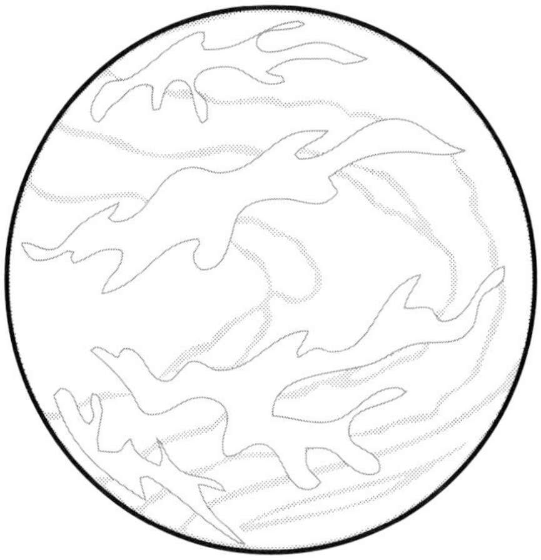

Distance from the Sun = _____

Number of moons = _____

Order of planet from the Sun = _____

1 year on Venus = _____ Earth days

1 day on Venus = this many Earth days/ hours _____

Interesting fact: _____

_____ ②

Earth
Color: water = blue,
land = brown, clouds = white

Distance from the Sun = _____

Number of moons = _____

Order of planet from the Sun = _____

1 year on Earth = _____ Earth days

1 day on Earth = this many Earth hours/ minutes _____

Interesting fact: _____

_____ ③

Note to the teacher: Use with "Pocket Planet Guides" on page 8.

Mars

Color: reddish orange

Distance from the Sun = _____

Number of moons = _____

Order of planet from the Sun = _____

1 year on Mars = _____ Earth days

1 day on Mars = this many Earth hours/
minutes _____

Interesting fact: _____

_____ ④

Jupiter

Color: planet = pink, red,
yellow, tan, white
Great Red Spot = dark red

Distance from the Sun = _____

Number of moons = _____

Order of planet from the Sun = _____

1 year on Jupiter = _____ Earth years

1 day on Jupiter = this many Earth hours/
minutes _____

Interesting fact: _____

_____ ⑤

Saturn

Color: planet = orange
rings = yellow

Distance from the Sun = _____

Number of moons = _____

Order of planet from the Sun = _____

1 year on Saturn = _____ Earth years

1 day on Saturn = this many Earth hours/
minutes _____

Interesting fact: _____

_____ ⑥

©2000 The Education Center, Inc. • *Investigating Science* • Solar System • TEC1745

10   **Note to the teacher:** Use with "Pocket Planet Guides" on page 8.

Uranus
Color: bluish green

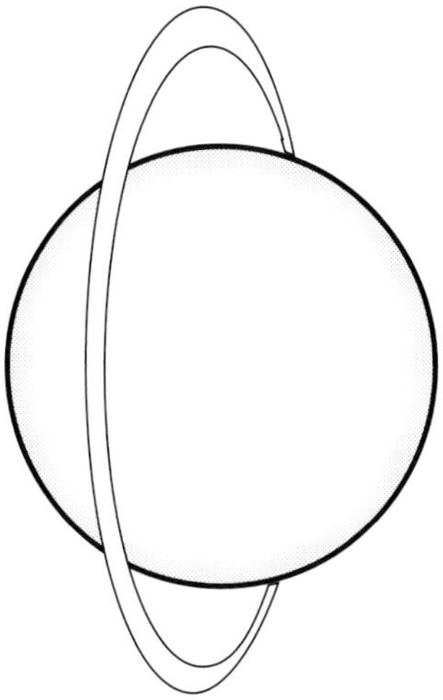

Distance from the Sun = _____

Number of moons = _____

Order of planet from the Sun = _____

1 year on Uranus = _____ Earth years

1 day on Uranus = this many Earth hours/ minutes _____

Interesting fact: _____

_____ ⑦

Neptune
Color: planet = blue
Great Dark Spot = dark blue

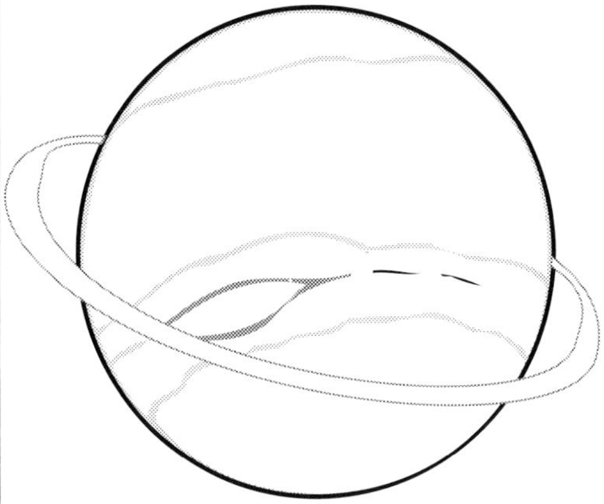

Distance from the Sun = _____

Number of moons = _____

Order of planet from the Sun = _____

1 year on Neptune = _____ Earth years

1 day on Neptune = this many Earth hours/ minutes _____

Interesting fact: _____

_____ ⑧

Pluto
Color: gray

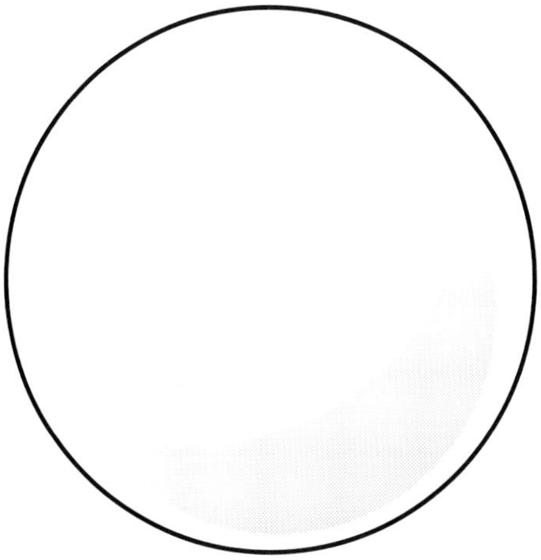

Distance from the Sun = _____

Number of moons = _____

Order of planet from the Sun = _____

1 year on Pluto = _____ Earth years

1 day on Pluto = this many Earth days/ hours _____

Interesting fact: _____

_____ ⑨

Comets, Meteors, and Stars

Use this collection of fun activities and reproducibles to turn your youngsters into stellar stargazers!

Background for the Teacher

- *Comets* are actually dirty balls of ice that orbit the Sun. Most comets have three parts: the *nucleus,* the *coma,* and the *tail.*
- The fuzzy white tail of a comet is created when the comet passes close to the Sun. The Sun's heat warms the comet and the thawed gas that steams away from it appears as a tail.
- *Meteoroids* are rocky fragments that orbit the Sun. If they enter Earth's atmosphere and burn up, they are called *meteors.* If they land on Earth, they are called *meteorites.*
- At least 25,000 years ago a large meteorite fell in the Arizona desert. It left a crater about $^3/_4$ mile (1.2 km) in diameter and more than 600 feet (200 m) deep.
- Stars are huge balls of hot, glowing gases.
- On a dark, clear night, you can see about 3,000 stars. If you look through a small telescope, you can see about 600,000 stars. Astronomers believe that there are at least 200 billion billion stars in space!

Meteorites
(Demonstration)

Introduce your students to the impact of meteorites with this gritty demonstration. Begin by reading aloud *Meteor!* by Patricia Polacco (Paper Star, 1996). This rollicking tale based on a true event will entertain students as it introduces them to meteorites. To demonstrate the impact of a meteorite, prepare a model of the Moon's surface by pouring sand into a pie pan. Add water to the sand until it is damp. Place the pan on the floor; then stand up and drop a potato into the pan. Carefully remove the potato and invite students to examine the impression it created in the sand.

Explain to students that meteors that enter Earth's atmosphere are usually no bigger than a grain of sand. Occasionally, however, larger meteors—now called meteorites—fall to Earth and leave a crater in the planet's surface. Many of the craters formed by meteorites are no longer visible because of the process of erosion. However, because the Moon doesn't have an atmosphere and erosion doesn't occur there, craters on the Moon remain visible for billions of years!

 A Star-Studded Literature Selection

Asteroids, Comets, and Meteors by Gregory L. Vogt (The Millbrook Press, Inc.; 1996)
How Many Stars in the Sky? by Lenny Hort (Mulberry Books, 1997)
The Magic School Bus Out of This World: A Book About Space Rocks by Joanna Cole (Scholastic Inc., 1996)
The Magic School Bus Sees Stars: A Book About Stars by Joanna Cole (Scholastic Inc., 1999)
Stars by Seymour Simon (Mulberry Books, 1989)

Where Do They Go?
(Demonstration)

Where do the stars go during the day? This simple demonstration will shed some light on that question! Make the classroom as dark as possible; then turn on a flashlight. Have the students observe the beam of light made by the flashlight. Next, turn the classroom lights on and shine the flashlight directly underneath an overhead light. Ask students if they can see the beam of light from the flashlight *(no)*. Then explain to students that the flashlight is like a star. At night, when there is no light from the Sun, we can see the stars shining brightly. However, during the day, the Sun's light is so bright that we cannot see the stars, even though they are still there.

Going Stargazing
(Preparation for Stargazing)

Star light, star bright, let's go watch the stars tonight! With a bit of preparation, students can have a fun and educational experience under the stars. Explain to your youngsters that looking at stars can be an overwhelming experience. With a star viewer, however, a person is able to look at and record one section of sky at a time. Next, inform each student that she's going to create her own star viewer. To begin, give each student a wire hanger. Instruct her to gently pull the hanger into a square shape. Then cover the sharp handle of each hanger with masking tape. Explain to the student that she will use her star viewer by holding it up and isolating part of the sky.

After the star viewers have been constructed, have each student make a stargazer journal. To create the journal, give each child a copy of page 16. Have her cut the booklet pages apart. Instruct her to stack the pages in numerical order with the cover on top. Then, to increase the number of journal pages, have her slip four 3" x 5" pieces of white paper behind journal page 2. Instruct her to staple her booklet along the left-hand side and decorate the cover as desired. Instruct each student to take her journal home and use it to record observations about the night sky.

Send a note home encouraging parents to take their children stargazing. In the note, direct the parent to read the checklist on page 1 of the child's stargazer journal for items to take on a stargazing adventure. Explain that putting a flashlight in a lunch sack will keep the light from being so bright that the child's eyes must readjust each time she looks from her book or journal back at the sky. Invite students to bring in their journals periodically to share their observations with the class.

A Stargazer's Journal

Name Tonya

A Celestial Constellation Viewer
(Viewing Constellations)

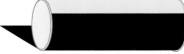

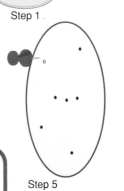

Bring the beauty of the night sky indoors with these out-of-this-world constellation viewers! Complete the first two steps for each child before passing out the materials. <u>Note</u>: The *Big Dipper* is not actually a constellation; rather it is an *asterism*, or a group of stars within a constellation. The Big Dipper is part of the constellation *Ursa Major*, or *Great Bear*.

Materials for each child:
1 empty Pringles® potato crisps can and lid
1 copy of page 17
1 thumbtack
2 sheets of 9" x 12" black construction paper
silver peel-and-stick stars, construction paper scraps, or sequins
glue
scissors

Directions:
1. Use the thumbtack to carefully pierce one hole in the center of the bottom of the can.
2. Use sharp scissors to cut out the center of the plastic lid as shown.
3. Wrap one sheet of black paper around the can and secure by gluing the overlapping edge. Decorate the can with stickers, paper scraps, or sequins.
4. Cut out the constellation circles on page 17. Put two or three small drops of glue on the back of each circle; then glue all six circles to the second sheet of black paper. Allow time for the glue to dry; then cut out each circle again.
5. Use the thumbtack to carefully pierce each star on each constellation circle.
6. To view a constellation, remove the lid from the can. Fit one circle inside the plastic lid so that the black side will face outside the can. Replace the lid, point the can toward a light source, and look through the hole at the bottom of the can. View each of the remaining constellations in the same manner.

Twinkle, Twinkle, Little Star
(Demonstration)

Why do stars appear to twinkle when the light of a star is actually steady? Demonstrate this phenomenon for students with a large glass bowl half full of water, a piece of aluminum foil, and a flashlight. Gently crumple the aluminum foil and place it on a flat surface. Place the bowl on top of the aluminum foil. When the water is still, darken the room and shine a flashlight into the bowl from above. Have students observe the light that is projected on the ceiling. Next, continue to shine the light into the bowl while gently tapping the surface of the water with your finger. Invite students to discuss the shimmering, twinkling results. Explain to your youngsters that because the light rays are *refracted,* or bent, the light appears to shimmer. In the same way, light rays from stars are bent as they travel through different air densities in Earth's atmosphere, producing twinkling stars.

14

Radiant Reflections
(Demonstration)

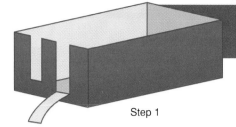

Step 1

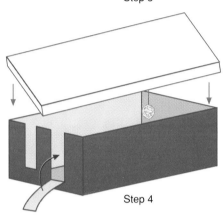

Step 3

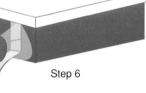

Step 4

Step 6

Unlike stars, comets don't produce their own light. Like the Moon, these celestial bodies reflect light from the Sun. Help students understand this concept with the following demonstration.

Materials:
1 shoebox with a lid
4" length of yarn
small piece of aluminum foil
flashlight
sharp scissors
tape

Directions:
1. Cut a deep, narrow flap on one end of the shoebox, about 1" from the side edge as shown. Next, cut a narrow hole on the same end of the box, about 1" from the opposite edge as shown.
2. Crumple the piece of foil around one end of the yarn so that it forms a ball about the size of a walnut.
3. Suspend the foil ball two inches from the end of the shoebox lid by taping it to the inside of the lid as shown.
4. Close the flap and place the lid on the box so that the foil ball is suspended near the uncut end of the box.
5. Have a student peer into the viewer and ask her to observe the foil ball. *(The ball should be barely visible, or not visible at all.)*
6. Remove the lid, open the flap, and replace the lid. Have the student peer into the box again while she shines a flashlight through the flap as shown. Have the student describe what she sees. *(When the light shines on the ball, it will appear to shine.)* Repeat the process, giving each student a chance to view the shining ball. Explain to students that this is similar to the way comets become visible in the night sky when they reflect the Sun's light.

Cosmic Comet Anatomy
(Making a Model)

Give students a hands-on lesson about the three parts of a comet with this model-making activity! Share with your students the information on the three parts of comets shown in the box below. Then have each child make his own comet using a Styrofoam® ball, an 18" x 18" white tissue paper square, and three cotton balls. Instruct the child to wrap the Styrofoam ball (the nucleus) in the center of the tissue paper so that the corners of the tissue paper make the comet's tail. Then have him gently stretch the cotton balls out and glue them to his comet to form the coma. Encourage each child to take his comet home and share his new knowledge of comets with his family.

Information About Comets
Most comets have three parts: the *nucleus,* the *coma,* and the *tail.* The nucleus, or the body of the comet, is an icy ball of dust and gas. The coma is a dusty cloud that forms around the nucleus as the comet's orbit brings it closer to the heat from the Sun. The comet's tail is formed when solar wind and radiation force the gases of the coma away from the Sun. The gases are swept behind the comet into a straight tail that can be as long as 90 million miles!

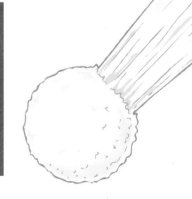

A Stargazer's Checklist

☐ Star Viewer

☐ Stargazer's Journal

☐ A pencil

☐ A book about stars or a planisphere

☐ A flashlight in a small lunch sack

☐ An old blanket

1

A Stargazer's Meteor Shower Calendar

Name	Date
Quadrantids	January 1–6
April Lyrids	April 19–24
Eta Aquarids	May 1–8
Delta Aquarids	July 15–August 15
Perseids	July 25–August 18
Orionids	October 16–27
Taurids	October 20–November 30
Leonids	November 15–20
Geminids	December 7–15

3

A Stargazer's Journal

Name _____

2

Date _____

Observations:

Note to the teacher: Use with "Going Stargazing" on page 13.

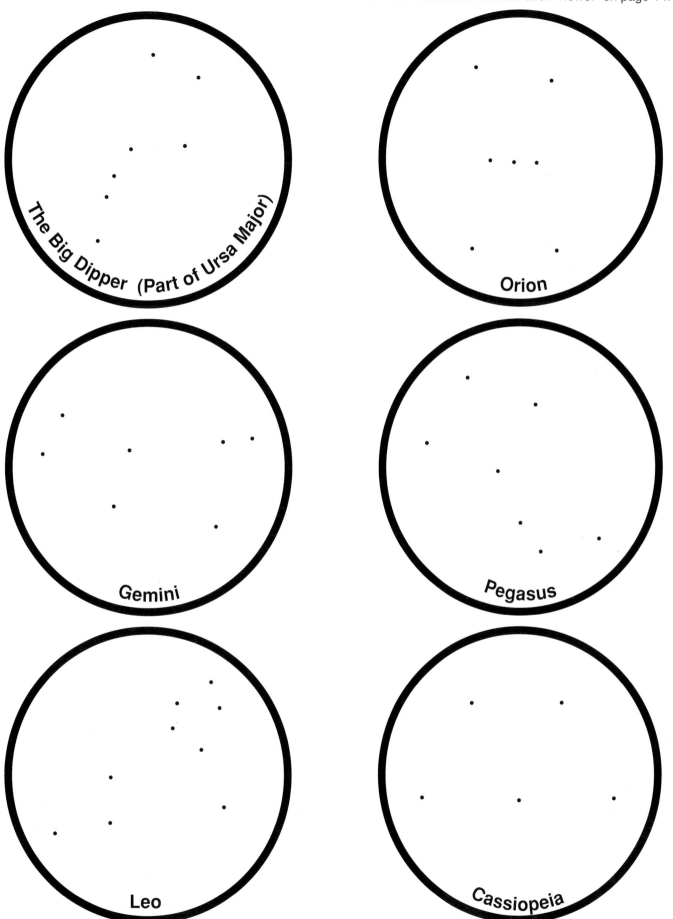

The Big Dipper (Part of Ursa Major)

Orion

Gemini

Pegasus

Leo

Cassiopeia

The Sun

Shed some light on the center of our solar system, the Sun, with this collection of ideas, activities, and reproducibles!

 ## Background for the Teacher

- The Sun is a medium-sized star.
- The Sun provides light and heat.
- The Sun plays an important part in the water cycle. The Sun's heat causes water to evaporate. The evaporated water eventually returns to Earth in the form of rain.
- Heat from the Sun warms the air on Earth and causes it to move, producing wind.
- The Sun measures 865,000 miles (1,392,000 km) across.
- The Sun is 5 billion years old.
- The Sun is the center of our solar system. The word *solar* means "about the Sun."
- Our Earth orbits around the Sun. It takes 365 days and 6 hours for Earth to complete one orbit. Once every four years, those six extra hours per year are put together to add one day to our year. When a year has 366 days in it, it's called a leap year.
- It is important never to look directly at the Sun, even while wearing sunglasses. The Sun's light is so strong that it can damage your eyes.

Sun Study
(Experiment)

It's tempting, but one should never look directly at the Sun. Studying the Sun's reflection is a safer way to get a look at the Sun. On a sunny day, divide the class into groups of three; then guide students through the activity.

Materials needed for each group:
mirror
pencil
1 sheet of yellow paper large enough to cover the mirror
one 9" x 12" sheet of white construction paper

Directions:
1. Use a pencil to carefully poke a hole in the center of the yellow paper.
2. Take the yellow paper, the mirror, and the white paper outside.
3. Have one member of the group place the yellow paper on top of the mirror and stand facing the Sun.
4. Have a second group member hold the white paper and stand with his back to the Sun about three feet away from the first group member.
5. Instruct the child holding the mirror to gently adjust the mirror until it reflects the Sun's image onto the white paper.
6. Direct the third group member to study the reflection of the Sun on the white paper.
7. Have the students change places and repeat the experiment until each child has had a turn looking at the Sun's reflection.

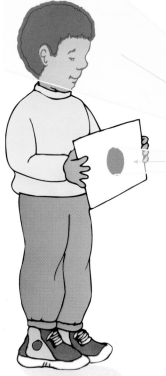

Bright, Shiny Books

Grandmother Spider Brings the Sun: A Cherokee Story by Geri Keams (Rising Moon, 1997)
Like Butter on Pancakes by Jonathan London (Puffin Books, 1998)
Rupa Raises the Sun by Marsha Wilson Chall (DK Publishing, 1998)
The Sun (Starting With Space series) by Paulette Bourgeois (Kids Can Press, 1997)
The Sun by Seymour Simon (William Morrow and Company, Inc.; 1986)

Sun Collage
(Art, Science)

Every living thing on Earth depends on the Sun. The Sun provides the heat, light, and energy that plants and animals need to survive. To reinforce this concept with your students, have each child make this radiant collage. Mount the completed collages on a bulletin board titled "We Depend on the Sun!"

Materials needed for each student:
one 9" x 12" sheet of orange construction paper
one 9" x 12" sheet of yellow construction paper
one 8" yellow construction paper circle
old magazines
scissors
glue

Directions:
1. Look through the magazines and cut out several small pictures of things that depend on the Sun to survive, such as plants, animals, and people. Glue the pictures in collage fashion onto the yellow circle.
2. To make the Sun's rays, cut six to eight long thin triangles from each sheet of construction paper.
3. Glue the triangles in a rotating color pattern around the outer edge of the circle as shown.

Why Do We Have Day and Night?
(Making a Booklet)

Have your students ever asked, "Where does the Sun go at night?" Making the following booklet will give students the answer to this question, as well as a bright reminder that the Sun provides daylight for everyone on Earth. In advance, cut several five-inch tagboard circle templates. Next, supply each student with the materials listed; then guide her through the steps to complete her booklet.

Materials for each student:
1 copy of page 22
one 6" x 6" piece of yellow construction paper
four 6" x 6" pieces of white construction paper
scissors
crayons or markers
access to a circle template and a stapler
glue

Directions:
1. Use the circle template and scissors to make one yellow circle and four white circles.
2. Cut out the Sun pattern on page 22 and color it orange. Cut out the four numbered cards on page 22.
3. Glue one numbered card to the bottom half of each white circle.
4. Read each card; then illustrate the card in the space above it.
5. Stack the white circles in order.
6. Place the yellow circle on top of the white circles. Staple the five circles to the center of the Sun pattern as shown.
7. Title the booklet "Why Do We Have Day and Night?"

19

Solar-Cooked S'mores
(Making a Solar Stove, Cooking)

Harness the Sun's energy and use it to cook up some chocolatey s'mores—no campfire required! Choose a warm, sunny day and have student volunteers help as you demonstrate the process for making a solar stove from a pizza box. Gather the supplies listed below and follow the directions to create a solar stove. (You may want to create more than one stove if you have a large number of students.) While you're making the stove, explain to the class that more than 300,000 homes in the United States use solar energy for heat. Homes that rely on solar energy use less fuel and less electricity than homes that do not.

After construction of the stove is complete, invite each student to use the recipe below to make her own solar-cooked s'mores. Be prepared for some lip-smackin' learning!

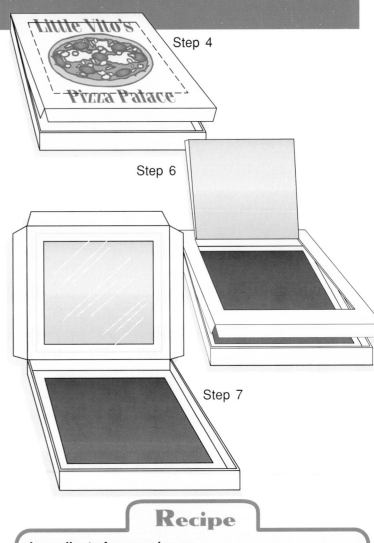

Step 4

Step 6

Step 7

Materials for one solar stove:
1 clean medium-sized pizza box
aluminum foil
black construction paper
clear plastic wrap
X-acto® knife
scissors
glue
tape
ruler
pencil

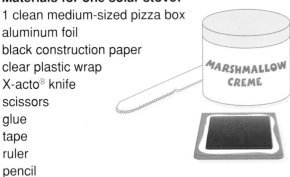

MARSHMALLOW CREME

Directions:
1. Cut a layer of aluminum foil to fit the inside bottom of the pizza box. Glue the aluminum foil in place.
2. Cover the aluminum foil with a layer of black construction paper cut to size. Glue the paper in place.
3. Close the box. With your ruler and a pencil, draw a two-inch border around the edge of the box top.
4. With the X-acto knife, cut three of the lines, as shown, to create a flap.
5. Hold a ruler firmly against the uncut line and have a student volunteer gently fold the flap back against the ruler.
6. Glue a layer of aluminum foil cut to size on the inside of the flap.
7. Open the box and tape a sheet of plastic wrap on the inside of the lid as shown.

Recipe

Ingredients for one s'more:
1 graham cracker square
spoonful of marshmallow creme
1/4 of a Hershey's® milk chocolate bar
plastic knife

Steps:
1. Spread the marshmallow creme on the graham cracker.
2. Place the chocolate piece on top of the marshmallow creme.
3. Open the solar stove and place the graham cracker on the black paper. Cover the bottom of the stove with s'mores, making sure that they don't touch and that they are all visible through the plastic cover when the oven top is closed.
4. Close the box lid and adjust the aluminum foil flap until the Sun's rays are directed onto the s'mores. A stick or pencil may be needed to prop the flap in the correct position.
5. Cook the s'mores for 15–20 minutes or until the chocolate is shiny.
6. Eat and enjoy!

Eclipse
(Simulation, Experiment)

A *solar eclipse* occurs when the Moon's shadow passes over Earth. How can the Moon block out the Sun when the Moon measures only about 2,160 miles (3,476 km) across and the Sun measures about 865,000 miles (1,392,000 km) across? Demonstrate this phenomenon for students with this quick experiment. Take the class outside and have students stand 25 to 35 feet away from a tall tree or another large object. Give each child a plastic checker. Have the child close her left eye and look at the tree with her right eye. Next, instruct the student to hold the checker in her right hand at arm's length, keep her left eye closed, and look at the tree. Then have her slowly bring the checker closer to her face until it is right in front of her eye. Have the student describe what happens. *(As the checker gets closer to her eye, it begins to block her view of the tree until she can't see the tree at all, even though the checker is much smaller than the tree.)* Explain to students that just like the checker blocks out the tree, the Moon is able to block our view of the Sun during a solar eclipse because the Moon is closer to Earth than the Sun is.

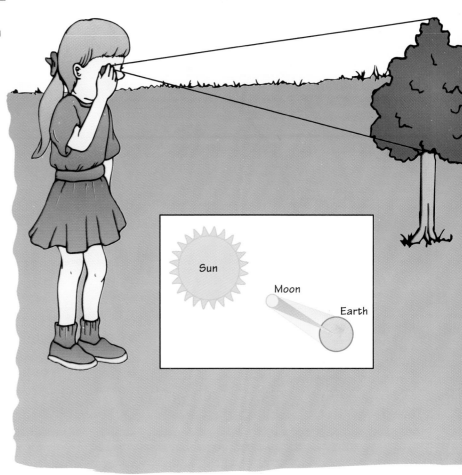

Sun Sense
(Health and Safety)

Impress upon students the importance of protecting themselves from the Sun's rays by making this Sun-savvy visor. Explain to the class that even on cloudy days the Sun's rays can be harmful. Sun damage can include sunburns, skin cancer, and eye damage. Have students discuss several methods of protecting themselves from the Sun, including wearing sunscreen, avoiding the Sun during its most intense hours (between 10 A.M. and 3 P.M.), and wearing protective clothing. Record their responses on chart paper. Next, inform each child that he is going to create his own protective Sun visor. Give each child a copy of page 23, one 12" x 1½" strip of construction paper, crayons or markers, scissors, and access to a stapler. Instruct each child to cut out his visor and write and illustrate on it several safety tips from the list. Staple one end of the strip to the visor, fit the visor to the child's head, and staple the other end. Take the class for a short walk outdoors and invite each student to sport his nifty new headgear. Now, that's Sun safety that will really go to their heads!

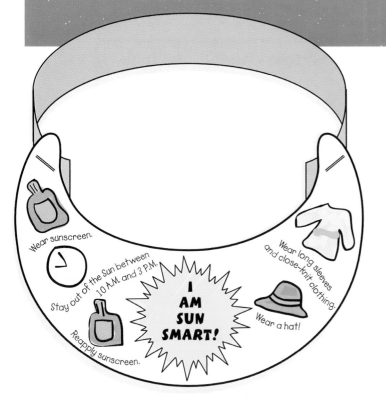

Pattern and Information Cards

Use with "Why Do We Have Day and Night?" on page 19.

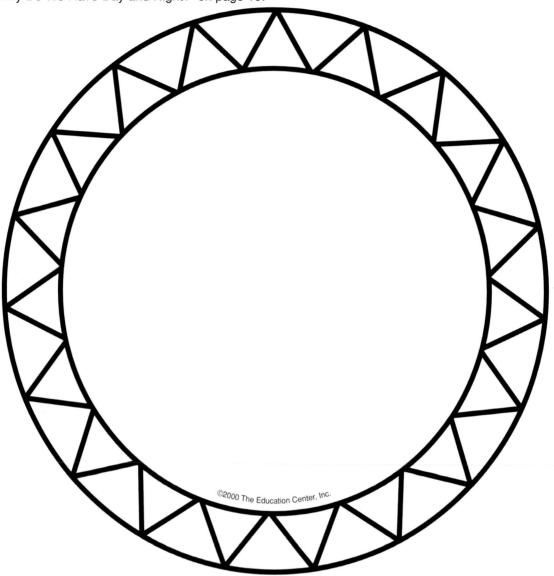

©2000 The Education Center, Inc.

1. Earth rotates as it orbits around the Sun.	2. When the part of Earth that you live on is facing the Sun, it is daytime where you live.
3. As the part of Earth that you live on rotates away from the Sun, it becomes nighttime where you live.	4. It takes one year, or 365 days, for Earth to complete its orbit around the Sun.

©2000 The Education Center, Inc. • *Investigating Science • Solar System* • TEC1745

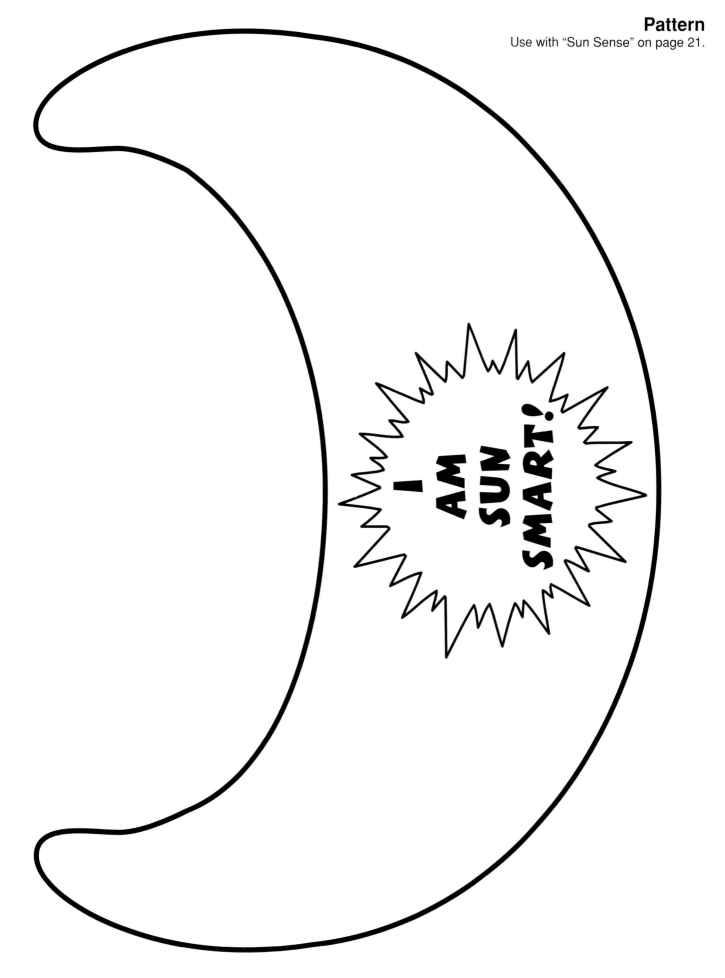

I AM SUN SMART!

The Moon

This collection of experiments and activities is sure to shed some light on the Moon for your students!

Earth

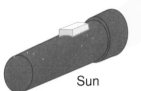

Moon

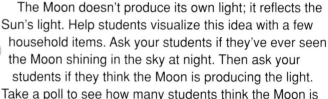

Sun

By the Light of the Silvery Moon
(Experiment)

The Moon doesn't produce its own light; it reflects the Sun's light. Help students visualize this idea with a few household items. Ask your students if they've ever seen the Moon shining in the sky at night. Then ask your students if they think the Moon is producing the light. Take a poll to see how many students think the Moon is producing the light and how many think the light comes from something else. Divide your students into groups of three. Provide each group with a flashlight, a mirror, and a ball. Next, instruct one member of each group to hold the flashlight, one member to hold the mirror, and one member to hold the ball. Then dim the lights and instruct each student holding the flashlight to shine it so that the light reflects off the mirror being held by the other group member. Direct the student holding the ball to position it so that it catches the light reflected off of the mirror. *(Remind students never to shine or reflect the light into other students' eyes.)* Inform your students that the flashlight is the Sun, the mirror is the Moon, and the ball is Earth. Next, ask your students if the Moon is creating the light that we see on Earth. *(No, the light is coming from the Sun and being reflected off the surface of the Moon.)* Then have each group repeat the process two more times so that each group member gets a chance to make moonlight.

Background for the Teacher

- The Moon is the only object that naturally orbits Earth.
- The Moon is about one-fourth the width of Earth.
- Much of the Moon's landscape is marked with *craters.* Craters are bowl-shaped depressions formed where meteorites have struck the surface.
- The Moon has two basic surface regions: rough, mountainous highlands and flat plains.
- The flat plains, called *maria,* are the dark spots we see on the Moon. Maria are believed to have been formed when meteorites struck the relatively young Moon hard enough to break the crust. Lava flowed into the craters and formed these plains as a result.
- The Moon's gravity is one-sixth of Earth's. Its gravitational pull creates the ocean tides.
- The Moon rotates once about every 27.3 days, and it revolves around Earth in the exact same period of time. Because of this, only one side of the Moon ever faces Earth.
- The Moon has little or no atmosphere and large temperature swings ranging from 260°F to –280°F.
- The observable portion of the sunlit Moon changes as the Moon revolves around Earth in relation to the Sun, creating different phases.
- A *lunar eclipse* (partial or total blockage of the Moon) occurs when the Moon travels through the shadow of Earth.

Marvelous Moon Books

The Best Book of the Moon by Ian Graham (Larousse Kingfisher Chambers, Inc.; 1999)

The Moon (Isaac Asimov's New Library of the Universe) by Isaac Asimov (Gareth Stevens Publishing, 1994)

The Moon (Starting With Space) by Paulette Bourgeois (Kids Can Press Ltd., 1999)

The Moon Book by Gail Gibbons (Holiday House, Inc.; 1998)

The Moon Seems to Change (Let's-Read-and-Find-Out Science®) by Franklyn Mansfield Branley (HarperTrophy, 1987)

Owl Moon by Jane Yolen (Philomel Books, 1987)

The Monthly Moon
(Reading, Listening, Creative Writing)

Since ancient times, many cultures have used the cycle from one new moon to the next to measure time. Inform your students that some Native American cultures use the pattern on a turtle's back as a calendar. According to these cultures, the 13 large scales found on the backs of some types of turtles stand for the 13 moons that some years have. (Other years have 12 moons.) Tell your students that many Native American cultures named these moons. Then read aloud *Thirteen Moons on Turtle's Back: A Native American Year of Moons* by Joseph Bruchac and Jonathan London (Paper Star, 1997). Together with your class, discuss why each cycle is named as it is. Then have your students rename the Moon of the current season. To do this, tell students to think about what is happening in nature, and have them creatively insert that event in the title of their Moon. To follow the pattern of the Native American stories, have students create their own myths or stories that tell how their Moon got its name. Have them write their stories on round, white pieces of paper. For an eye-catching display, post on a bulletin board an enlarged copy of the turtle pattern on page 29. Title the display "The Moons on Turtle's Back." Then post each student's story around the pattern.

Man in the Moon
(Art, Creative Thinking)

Can you see the man in the Moon? The Moon's darker spots are sometimes imagined to be the shape of something, just as clouds are imagined to resemble objects or animals. Tell your students that people all over the world see shapes of people or animals in the Moon. Some people see a man, some a rabbit, and some Jack and Jill. Next, inform your students that the dark spots on the Moon are called *maria*. They are believed to have been formed when meteorites struck the relatively young Moon hard enough to break its crust, causing lava to flow up into the craters and form these plains. To help students create their own creatures in the Moon, gather the materials listed and follow the steps below.

Materials:
dishpan full of water
chalk
plastic knife
1 black construction paper circle (8" diameter) for each student
one 6" x 6" sheet of white paper for each student
newspaper
glue
string
access to a hole puncher

1. Man
2. Dog
3. Dragon
4. Ship

Steps:
1. Give each student one black construction paper circle and one 6" x 6" sheet of white paper.
2. Have the student use the plastic knife to carefully shave chalk onto the surface of the water. *(For safety reasons, complete Step 2 for younger students.)*
3. Instruct the student to gently and quickly dip her circle into the chalk and water mixture and then set the pattern on a sheet of newspaper to dry.
4. After the circle has dried, have the student examine one side of the pattern and look for shapes or images created by the chalk and water. Then have her list on the white square of paper all the people, animals, or other images that she can see in her Moon.
5. Have her glue the list to the unexamined side of the circle.
6. Punch a hole at the top of the circle. Tie a length of string through the hole. Hang the finished products from the ceiling for an out-of-this-world display!

The Great Disappearing Act!
(Demonstration)

Have your youngsters ever wondered why the Moon seems to change shapes? Use the following simple activity to help illustrate the Moon's phases for your students. Divide your class into small groups. To complete the activity, supply each group with the materials listed and follow the steps shown.

Materials for each group:
1 large, dark-colored ball such as a basketball or kick ball
1 large flashlight
1 sticky note

Demonstration Steps:
1. Instruct one person in each group to hold the flashlight.
2. Instruct a second person in each group to place the sticky note on one side of the ball. Then have him hold the ball up and away from his body so that the sticky note is facing him and he is looking up a little to see the ball.
3. Instruct the student with the flashlight to stand in front (a few feet away) of the student holding the ball. Have the student shine the light on the student holding the ball.
4. Explain to students that the flashlight represents the Sun, the ball represents the Moon, and the head of the student holding the ball is Earth. Further explain that the sticky note stuck to the ball is simply a reminder that the same side of the Moon always faces Earth.
5. Turn off the lights. Point out to the student that the ball (the Moon) should be dark on the side he sees. Inform the student that this is a *new moon.*
6. Have the student slowly turn counterclockwise until he sees a small sliver of light on the ball. (Remind the student to always keep the sticky note in front of him.) Inform the student that this is a *crescent moon.*
7. Instruct the student to continue turning until he sees a little more of the ball illuminated. Inform the student that this is a *first-quarter moon.*
8. Direct the student to continue turning until all of the side he can see is illuminated. Inform the student that this is a *full moon.*
9. Have the student keep turning. Point out that less and less of the ball will be illuminated. Have him stop when about three-fourths of the ball is dark. Inform him that this is the *third-quarter* or *last-quarter moon.*
10. Instruct the student to keep turning until he sees another *crescent moon* and then once again no moon or the *new moon.*
11. Ask the students if the ball ever decreased in size as the student rotated. *(No)* Then have your students explain what did change that made the Moon appear to change shapes. *(The amount of visible sunlight hitting the moon changed, making it only appear to change shapes.)*

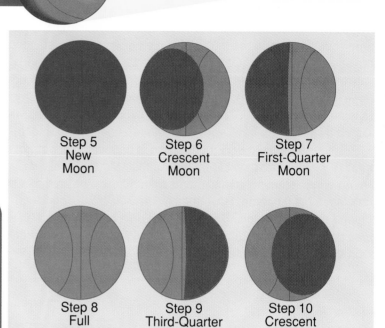

Step 5
New
Moon

Step 6
Crescent
Moon

Step 7
First-Quarter
Moon

Step 8
Full
Moon

Step 9
Third-Quarter
Moon

Step 10
Crescent
Moon

Extraordinary Eclipse
(Experiment)

Did you say a lunar eclipse saved Christopher Columbus? Tell your students that Columbus once saved himself and his crew by predicting a *lunar eclipse* (when the Moon moves out of the Sun's light and into Earth's shadow). This prediction frightened the islanders into feeding him and his crew.

Help students understand how a lunar eclipse occurs with this simple experiment. You'll need one shadeless lamp (the Sun) and a ball (the Moon) for each group of students. Place the shadeless lamp at head level in the center of a dark room. *(Remind students not to touch the lightbulb or look directly at it.)* Divide the class into groups and give each group a ball. Position the groups around the lamp. Have one student from each group hold the ball at arm's length and at eye level. Position the student so that the ball is pointed toward the light. Ask your students to predict what will happen to the Moon if the student (Earth) begins to slowly turn. Record their responses on the board. Then instruct each student holding a ball to slowly turn in place, keeping the ball at arm's length and at eye level. Ask the other group members to observe what happens. *(The student's head [Earth] blocks the lamp's light [the Sun], casting a shadow on the ball [the Moon]).*

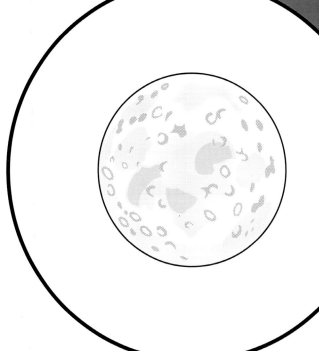

Lunar Illusion
(Experiment)

Which is bigger, the Moon or the star twinkling next to it? Pair students to complete the following simple experiment to see how the Moon fools us into thinking it's bigger than the stars. In advance, make a copy of the circle patterns shown for each pair. Cut out the center pattern (the Moon), leaving each group with a larger circular frame and the Moon. To begin the experiment, give each pair one set of patterns. Then guide each pair through the steps below to complete the experiment. After the experiment, ask your class how the size of the Moon compared with the frame at 5 and 20 feet. Ask them if the Moon changed size. Explain that the added distance only made the Moon appear to get smaller. Then explain that in reality the stars are much farther from Earth than the Moon is, so they appear much smaller. The Moon isn't so tricky after all!

Steps:
1. Have one person hold the frame at arm's length in her line of vision. Direct the second person to stand five feet away and hold up the small circle pattern (the Moon.)
2. Instruct the partner with the frame to view the Moon through the frame, noting its size.
3. Repeat the experiment, having the student with the Moon stand 20 feet away.
4. Have students in each pair switch roles and repeat the experiment.

One Small Step for Man, One Giant Leap for Mankind
(Timeline)

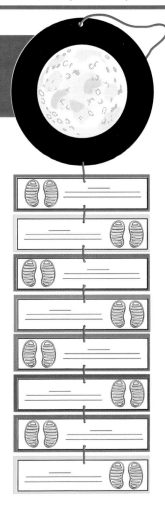

Imagine walking in the footsteps of the men who first explored the Moon! Tell students that the journey toward understanding the Moon began in ancient times with observations made by the naked eye and continues to this day with specialized telescopes and probes. Help your students travel the path of discovery by creating Moon exploration timelines. Divide your students into pairs. Give each pair the supplies listed; then guide the pair through the steps below to create a timeline. Hang the completed timelines in your classroom and use them as references throughout your study of space.

Materials for each pair:
1 copy each of pages 30 and 31
8 colorful construction paper strips (2" x 7")
1 black construction paper circle (6" diameter)
scissors
8 lengths of yarn
glue
hole puncher
access to reference materials on the Moon's explorations

Steps:
1. Cut out the Moon pattern and the eight date strips on pages 30 and 31.
2. Glue each date strip onto one colored construction paper strip. Then glue the Moon pattern to the center of the black construction paper circle.
3. Punch holes in the Moon pattern and date strips where indicated by the black holes.
4. Put the cards in order by date. Then use a length of yarn to connect the most recent date strip to the bottom of the Moon. Use the other lengths of yarn to tie the remaining date strips in order, ending with the earliest Moon date strip.

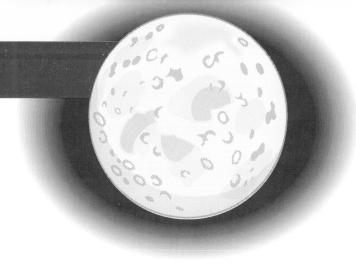

The Moon Festival
(Reading, Art)

The Chinese have a legend or fairy tale for many things, including the Moon. The Chinese planted and harvested by the Moon. Because of this, they have included the Moon in times of worship. Each year, the 15th day of the eighth lunar month has been a traditional holiday called the Moon Festival or the Mid Autumn Festival. The Tang dynasty (A.D. 618–906) made this an official holiday. The 15th day of the eighth lunar month usually falls during the month of August, September, or October. To introduce your students to the tradition of the Moon Festival, read aloud *Moon Festival* by Ching Yeung Russell (Boyd Mills Press, 1997). *(Another wonderful book to share with students about the Moon Festival is* The Moon Lady *by Amy Tan [Aladdin Paperbacks, 1995].)* After reading the story, tell your students that lanterns made from colorful waxed paper are an important part of the celebration. Have each student create her own waxed-paper lantern by following the directions below. To culminate the activity and your study of the Moon, hold your own Moon Festival. Hang each student's lantern in your classroom and serve some traditional Chinese Moon Festival foods, such as chicken, roast pork, moon cakes, and fruits such as grapefruit, star fruit, and persimmons.

Materials for each student:
1 sheet of waxed paper 44" long
access to 4 different colors of bottled colored glue
four 2' lengths of yarn
access to hole puncher
access to stapler

Step 1

Steps 2–3

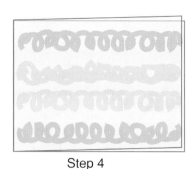

Step 4

Steps 5–8

Directions:
1. Fold the sheet of waxed paper as shown and crease the fold. Then unfold the paper.
2. Select a color of glue and, beginning at the top to the right of the fold line, make a squiggle line of glue the length of the waxed paper half as shown.
3. Repeat the process with each color of glue, creating one colored squiggle line underneath the other until the entire half is filled.
4. Carefully fold the left half over, matching the two ends of the paper and firmly pressing the two layers together as shown.
5. To create the lantern, bend the paper around until the two ends overlap about an inch. Staple the top and bottom of each end to secure.
6. Hole-punch four holes in the top of the lantern as shown.
7. Insert one length of yarn into each hole and tie to secure as shown.
8. Gather the four free ends of the strings and tie into one knot.

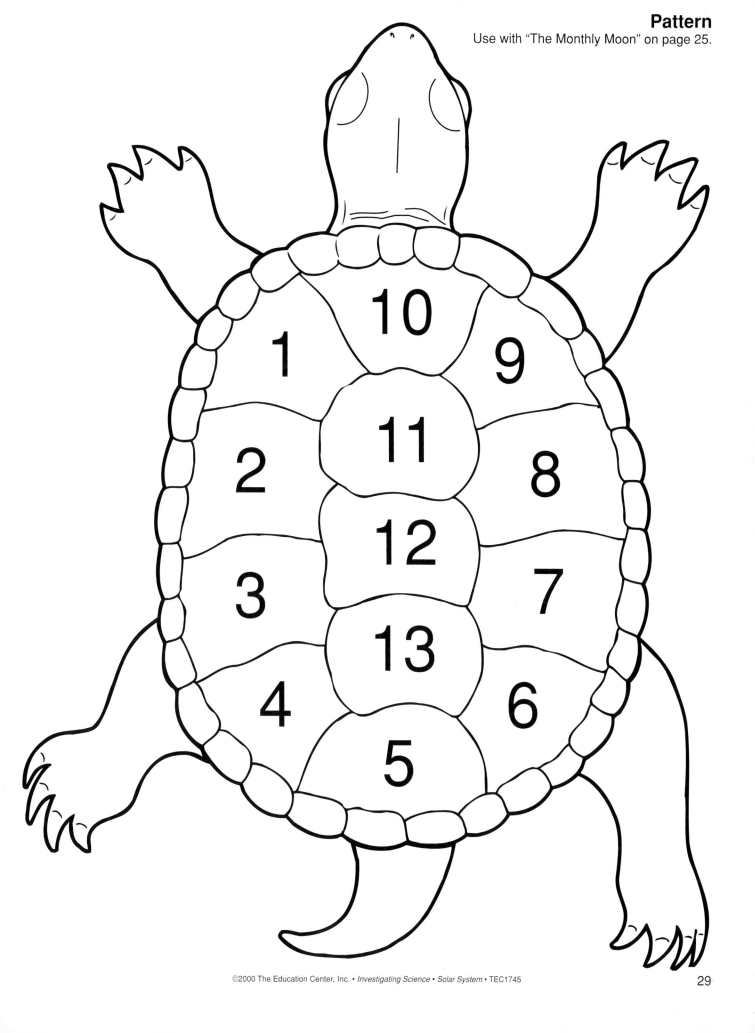

Patterns
Use with "One Small Step for Man,
One Giant Leap for Mankind" on page 27.

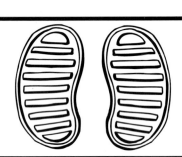

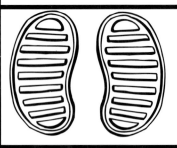

1687
**Sir Isaac Newton explains the Moon's motion
and its effect on Earth's tides.**

1957
Soviet Union launches *Sputnik 1.*

1966
**Soviet Union's *Luna 9* becomes the first
spacecraft to make a soft landing on the
Moon.**

1965
First American space walk occurs.

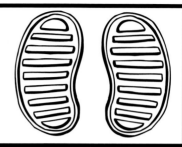

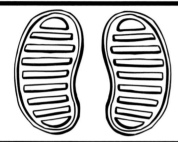

1969
***Apollo 11* astronaut Neil Armstrong becomes the first man to walk on the Moon.**

1968
***Apollo 8* astronauts orbit the Moon ten times.**

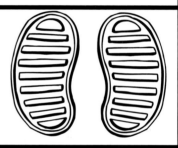

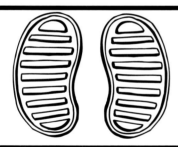

1962
John Glenn becomes the first American to orbit Earth.

1609–1610
Galileo uses a telescope to study the Moon.

Earth

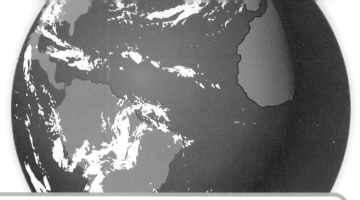

Take an educational ride on planet Earth with this selection of activities and reproducibles sure to inspire your young learners.

Background for the Teacher

- Earth revolves around the Sun about once every 365 days.
- Earth's orbit around the Sun creates the seasons. For several months each year half of Earth is tilted toward the Sun, receiving maximum sunlight (summer); the other half is tilted away, receiving minimum sunlight (winter).
- Earth makes one complete rotation on its axis each day (about every 24 hours). During this continuous rotation, half of Earth is facing the Sun and experiencing daytime while the other half is experiencing nighttime.
- *Gravity* is the force of attraction between objects.
- Earth consists of three layers: the *crust,* the *mantle,* and the *core.*
- Earth's crust is broken into nearly 30 plates that float on a layer of very hot rock. Earthquakes occur when the plates break and shift.
- Earth's water supply has been recycled countless times.
- Water in the air around us is called *water vapor.*
- Air takes up space and has weight.

Down-to-Earth Books

The Magic School Bus® Inside the Earth by Joanna Cole (Scholastic Inc., 1989)
On the Day You Were Born by Debra Frasier (Harcourt Brace & Company, 1991)
Our Planet Earth by Claire Llewellyn (Scholastic Inc., 1997)
You're Aboard Spaceship Earth by Patricia Lauber (HarperTrophy, 1996)

Earth on the Move
(Making a Banner)

Reveal the mystery of seasonal change by reading *The Reasons for Seasons* by Gail Gibbons (Holiday House, Inc.; 1996). This book takes your students on the yearlong journey of Earth's orbit around the Sun. After reading the book, direct pairs of students to act out Earth's rotation and its revolution around the Sun. Have one student represent the Sun, while the other student, Earth, rotates counterclockwise and revolves counterclockwise around the Sun. Have the students stop each quarter of the revolution to state the name of a different season, remembering to say the seasons in order. Now have youngsters complete an open-ended banner that gives insight into their perception of the seasons. Make one copy of page 37 for each child. Instruct the child to cut the banner sections apart along the bold lines. Then have the student glue page 3 to page 2 as shown. Direct the child to complete each sentence on the banner and then draw a picture that reflects his thoughts for each sentence. Invite the children to color the pictures. Display the banners on a bulletin board titled "Seasonal Thoughts."

From Day to Night
(Demonstration)

Help your students understand night and day with a simple turn of a globe. In advance, gather a globe, a flashlight, and a small sticker. Begin by putting the sticker on the globe to indicate where you live. Place the globe on a table; then dim the lights in your classroom. Have a student shine the flashlight on the globe, illuminating your home (the sticker). Ask students if it looks like day or night where the sticker is located *(day)*. Turn the globe counterclockwise, illuminating the other side. Students will notice that the sticker is now on the darker side of the globe, which represents nighttime. Now repeat the process and have students identify countries that experience night at the same time they, the students, are experiencing day.

Pulled by Gravity
(Experiment, Recording Data)

Use this activity to show your students how gravity keeps them grounded. Explain that gravity is the force that pulls objects toward the center of Earth. Light objects and heavy objects fall at the same speed unless air resistance slows them down. Divide the students into small groups. Direct each group to investigate the force of gravity on various objects by observing their fall to Earth and then recording the data on a chart like the one shown. Have each group gather several objects, such as a pencil, a marker, an eraser, a penny, a tissue, a book, a paper clip, and a piece of paper. Instruct the group to select a pair of objects, then drop each object at the same time from the same height. Have the group observe the objects' fall and then record the outcome. Instruct the group to repeat this process with the remaining objects and record the results. Have each group report its findings to the rest of the class. Guide your students into seeing that most pairs of objects dropped reached the ground at approximately the same time. If a group had a pair of objects that did not reach the ground at the same time, such as a tissue and a book, have the class discuss why this occurred. *(Both items encountered air resistance, but the tissue acted more like a parachute, slowing its fall.)*

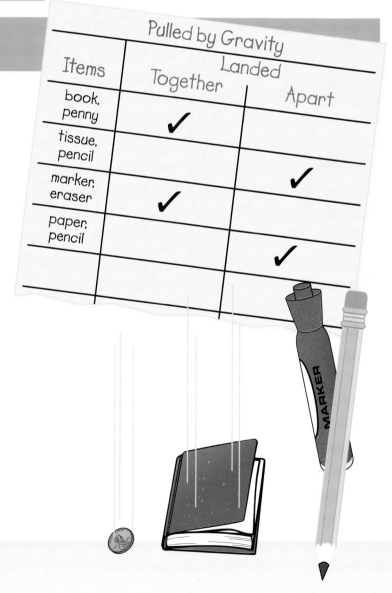

Items	Pulled by Gravity Landed Together	Apart
book, penny	✔	
tissue, pencil		
marker, eraser	✔	✔
paper, pencil		
		✔

Inside Earth

(Completing a Diagram, Making an Edible Model)

Take an inside look at Earth's layers with this tasty activity. In advance, make a class supply of page 38. Then write on a sheet of chart paper the Earth Facts shown or make a transparency of the information. Discuss the facts with your students. Next, distribute one copy of page 38 to each child. Instruct the student to use the facts to help her label and color the diagram of Earth's layers on page 38.

Culminate the activity and reinforce students' understanding of the layers of our planet by having students use the recipe shown to create Earth Pops. Have each student bite into her Earth Pop on your signal. Next, have her identify each layer (core, mantle, crust). Then let your students enjoy eating the rest of their creations.

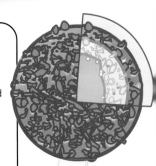

Directions:
1. Insert the craft stick into the center of the gumdrop (core).
2. Flatten the Rice Krispies Treats® bar (mantle); then mold it around the gumdrop.
3. Put the two sections of chocolate graham cracker in the plastic bag; then crush to make crumbs.
4. Place the Earth Pop in the bag with the crumbs and gently shake to evenly distribute the crumbs (crust). Press the chocolate crumbs to the pop before removing it from the bag.

Earth Facts

- Earth's layers are the *crust,* the *mantle,* and the *core.*
- The outer layer is called the crust. This thin rock layer and the water covering are home to all known living things on Earth.
- The layer beneath the crust is called the mantle. The mantle is a thick layer of soft molten rock.
- At the center of Earth is the core, a metallic ball made of iron and nickel.

Shake, Rattle, and Record

(Making an Instrument)

Your young scientists will be quakin' in their boots when they discover they'll be making and using seismographs. Explain to your students that Earth's crust consists of about 30 plates that fit together like a puzzle. These plates float, shift, and collide on top of Earth's mantle layer. Further explain that because of these movements the area between the plates, called a *fault,* becomes stressed, causing the rock to break and shift. When this happens an earthquake occurs. Then tell your students that a *seismograph* is an instrument that records the movement of the ground. Scientists use seismographs to determine the location and measure the strength of an earthquake. Next, have your students work in groups to make seismographs and record tremors in the classroom. Distribute the materials listed and follow the steps to complete the activity.

Materials for each group:
1 compass
2 pencils
1 roll of adding machine tape

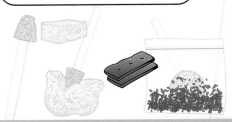

Steps:
1. Have one student in each group slip a pencil through the roll of adding machine tape. Direct the student to hold the roll of tape at one end of the desk. Then instruct the student to keep the roll steady by holding the pencil on each end.
2. Have the second student pull the end of the paper to the opposite end of the desk while the first student continues to hold the roll stationary. Then have the third student hold the compass so the pencil just touches the paper's surface.
3. Instruct the fourth student to gently bump the side of the desk to cause a tremor while the second student slowly pulls the adding machine paper.
4. Have the group observe the recorded movement of the desk made by the pencil on the paper.
5. Direct students to observe what happens when the fourth student bumps the desk more intensely. *(The recorded movement on the adding machine tape is more jagged and sporadic.)*

The Water Cycle
(Demonstration)

Could our water supply ever be used up? The answer is no. Inform your youngsters that the water we use today has been reused over and over. Also explain that every drink of water we take contains molecules of water that have been used many times before. Next, tell your youngsters that this is all possible because of a process called *the water cycle.* Use the following demonstration to help your students better understand how water is recycled. In advance, gather the materials listed and then follow the steps below. Follow up the demonstration by having each child complete a copy of page 39.

Materials needed:
teakettle
water
pie pan
ice cubes
access to a stove or heating element

Steps:
Warning: Keep students away from all electrical appliances and cords. Do *not* have students assist with this demonstration. Recruit a parent volunteer to assist.

1. Boil water in a teakettle until steam appears. Point out the steam and explain to students that as water boils, it evaporates into the air and becomes water vapor.
2. Place several ice cubes in the pie pan and hold it over the steam. Tell students that when the water vapor reaches the cool pie pan, the vapor will condense (become water droplets) on the bottom of the pan. Explain to your youngsters that when water vapor condenses into droplets of liquid in the sky, clouds form.
3. Have the students continue to watch the bottom of the pan until the droplets become too heavy and fall from the pan. Explain to students that a similar thing occurs in the clouds. When the droplets in a cloud become too heavy, they fall to the ground as rain.

Moist Air
(Experiment)

Help your youngsters quench their thirsts as well as learn about water in the air with the following activity. In advance, gather one plastic cup, several ice cubes, and a serving of colored fruit juice for each student. Explain to students that even though we can't see it, there is water in the air in the form of water vapor. Give each child one cup of juice with ice cubes. Have her observe the outside of the cup for several minutes. When droplets form on the outside of the cup, instruct her to wipe some of the water off the exterior of the cup and then inspect the color. Point out to your students that the drops are clear, unlike the juice inside the cup. Explain that the water droplets on the outside of the cup formed because the temperature of the cup is colder than the air around it. This causes water vapor in the air to condense, or change to water droplets, on the exterior of the cup. Culminate the activity by having students drink their juice and think about this chilling discovery!

Air Has Weight
(Investigation)

Not only does air take up space, but it has weight as well. Have students test this fact by creating a balloon balance. Divide the students into pairs. Gather the materials listed and follow the steps below.

Materials for each pair:
2 balloons
three 1' lengths of string
ruler
tape

Steps:
1. Tape one length of string to the center of the ruler as shown. Then tape the remaining two lengths of string one inch from each end of the ruler.
2. Fully inflate one balloon and then tie it to a string at one end of the ruler.
3. Barely inflate the second balloon; then tie it to the string at the opposite end of the ruler.
4. Ask the students to hypothesize what will happen when they test the balloon balance.
5. Hold the balloon balance by the string taped to the center of the ruler and wait for movement to stop. *(The fully inflated balloon is heavier, causing the end of the ruler to dip slightly.)*

Takin' Up Space
(Investigation, Art)

Does air take up space? Use this simple balloon activity to prove to your students that air does in fact take up space. In advance, gather a class set of balloons and paper cups. Begin by explaining to students that Earth is unique because our atmosphere is made of a layer of air. This layer of air occupies space for about 1,000 miles above Earth. Then give each child a deflated balloon and ask him to tell you what is inside the balloon. Next, have the child blow air into the balloon to inflate it. (Youngsters will realize that the air blown into the balloon takes up the space inside.) Have the student place one hand near the opening of his balloon and then release some of the air from the balloon. Have students describe what they feel *(the air taking up space inside the balloons suddenly rushes out)*. To help each child remember that air takes up space, have him create an Airhead character. Instruct each student to reinflate his balloon and then tie a knot at the opening. Have him tape the balloon to the top of a paper cup as shown. Then direct the student to carefully add facial features using items such as stickers, markers, yarn, pom-poms, or construction paper. Have each child share his Airhead character with the rest of the class.

Spring

In spring, I _____
_____
_____ . 1

Summer

In summer, I _____
_____
_____ . 2

Name

Fall

In fall, I _____
_____
_____ . 3

Glue to page 2.

Winter

In winter, I _____
_____
_____ . 4

Name _____

Inside Earth

Use the clues below to help you label Earth.
Use the code on the Moon to color each part of Earth.

Color Code

crust = brown
mantle = orange
core = red
water = blue
land = green

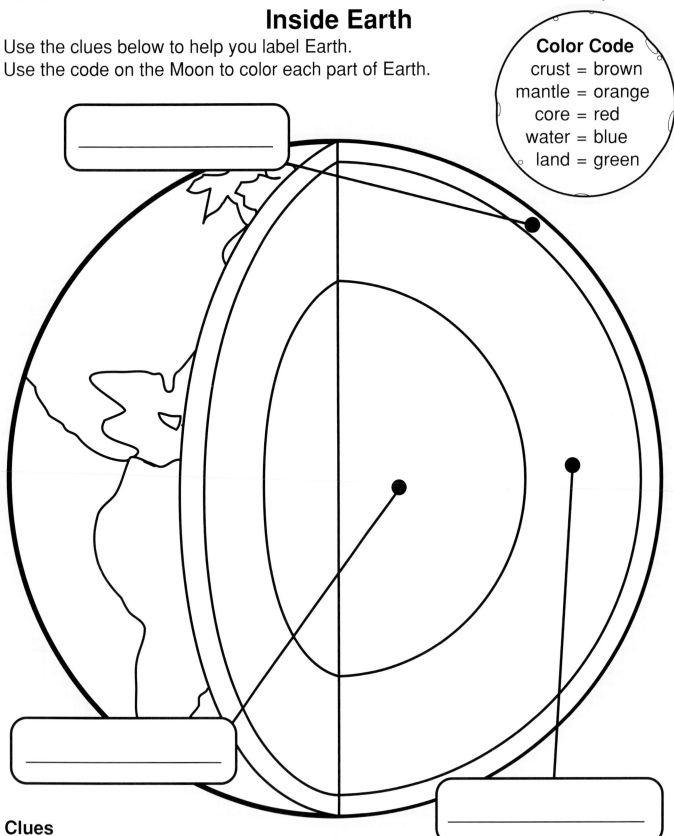

Clues

1. The **mantle** is between the crust and the core.
2. We live on the outer layer called the **crust.**
3. The **core** is found in the center of Earth.

©2000 The Education Center, Inc. • *Investigating Science* • *Solar System* • TEC1745

Note to the teacher: Use with "Inside Earth" on page 34.

The Water Cycle

Use the clues to label each stage of the water cycle.

Clues

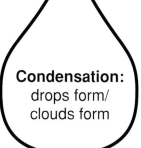

Evaporation:
vapor rises

Condensation:
drops form/
clouds form

Precipitation:
drops fall

- -

Note to the teacher: Use with "The Water Cycle" on page 35.

Space Travel

Reach for the stars with this collection of engaging, hands-on activities and reproducibles aimed at space travel.

What's Been Up There?
(Making a Timeline)

Use the following creative timeline activity to help your students better understand when the different types of spacecrafts were first launched. Give your students a brief history of the U.S. space program. Then have each student make a timeline highlighting some important U.S. spacecrafts. Provide each student with the materials listed below; then guide the students through the directions. Display the completed rocket timelines on a bulletin board titled "What's Been Up There?"

Materials for each student:
1 copy each of pages 44 and 45, one 12" x 18" sheet of black construction paper, one 9" x 12" sheet of red construction paper, ruler, scissors, glue, markers or crayons

Directions:
1. Fold the large sheet of construction paper in half vertically. Use a ruler to divide the paper into eight sections, each about 2¼ inches wide. Cut the front half of the folded construction paper into eight flaps as shown.
2. Cut out along the bold lines the illustrations on page 44 and the spacecraft fact cards on page 45. Read each fact card; then pair it with the correct illustration. Arrange each pair in order from the earliest date to the latest date.
3. Beginning with the earliest spacecraft, glue each illustration on one outer flap of the folded construction paper. Then glue each matching fact card on the space underneath each flap as shown.
4. Use the red sheet of construction paper to create a top and bottom for the timeline, making it resemble a rocket.

Background for the Teacher

- Traveling to outer space became a reality in 1961.
- A rocket is needed to lift any object up into space. As many as two rockets per week are launched into space across the world.
- In 1981 the United States built the world's first reusable spacecraft, the space shuttle.
- A space shuttle is launched like a rocket, then returns to Earth like a plane.
- The first "astronauts" sent into space were animals. Among the first: a dog named Laika in 1957 and a chimpanzee named Ham in 1961.
- On July 20, 1969, an American named Neil Armstrong became the first person to walk on the Moon.
- In space astronauts perform science experiments, repair and maintain the spacecraft, and deploy satellites.
- In 1998 the International Space Station began being assembled in 16 different nations around the world. Completion is expected in 2004.

Space Travel Tales

Astronauts Today by Rosanna Hansen (Random House, Inc.; 1998)
Floating in Space (Let's-Read-and-Find-Out Science® series) by Franklyn M. Branley (HarperCollins Publishers, Inc.; 1998)
I Am an Astronaut by Cynthia Benjamin (Barron's Educational Series, Inc.; 1996)
One Giant Leap (An Owlet Book) by Mary Ann Fraser (Henry Holt and Company, Inc.; 1999)
Space Explorer Atlas by Richard Platt (Dorling Kindersley Publishing, Inc.; 1999)

Airplanes...

- are built to fly through air
- have wings to help them stay in the air as gravity tries to pull them down
- have a streamlined or special shape that helps them move through the air
- sometimes have jet engines capable of flying 2,000 miles per hour

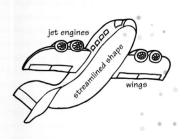

jet engines

streamlined shape

wings

Rockets...

- are sometimes built to fly through the air and then up into space
- don't need wings to help keep them up because there is no gravity in space
- use the most powerful engines ever built to help them fly fast enough (about 17,000 miles per hour) to get up into space
- have streamlined nose tips to help them cut through Earth's air before they reach space

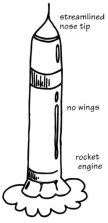

streamlined nose tip

no wings

rocket engine

Finding Out About Flight
(Critical Thinking)

Ever wonder why airplanes can't fly into space? Use the following activity to help your students discover the answer. Begin by explaining that a scientist makes a guess, based on facts, about what she thinks will happen or why something did happen. Tell your students that this guess is called a *hypothesis*. Next, divide your students into small groups and provide each group with three sheets of paper and markers. Instruct each group to label the top of one sheet "airplanes" and the top of the other "rockets." Direct group members to work together to list as many facts about these flying machines as possible. Then have the group use these facts to write on its third sheet of paper a hypothesis on why airplanes can't fly into space but rockets can. Have each group read its hypothesis to the class. Then prepare and display a transparency of the airplane/rocket information shown. Read aloud each description. Next, have each group star on its list any facts that also were listed on the transparency. Then direct the group to cross off of its list any information that isn't a fact. Next, help the group revise its hypothesis and write it on a strip of poster board. Post these on a bulletin board titled "Why Can't Airplanes Fly Into Space?"

Space Station Construction
(Making a Model)

Use this model-making activity to help your students understand the important features of the International Space Station (ISS). Explain to students that 16 countries, including the United States, are working together to build the ISS, where astronauts and scientists can work and live. Further explain that the construction began in 1998 and is to be completed in 2004. Once completed, the ISS will be about as tall as a 20-story building, wider than a football field, and contain up to 100 rooms called *modules*. Write on a sheet of chart paper the five important parts of a space station (as shown). Discuss each item and its importance to the astronauts. Then tell your students that they are going to work in pairs to create space station models. Provide the suggested materials listed below. Instruct each pair to include and label the five space station parts on its model. As students work, remind them that they may need to alter the design of their models to make them more balanced or to accommodate more modules. Set aside time for each pair to describe its model and features. Then secure a length of string around each space station and hang the models from the ceiling.

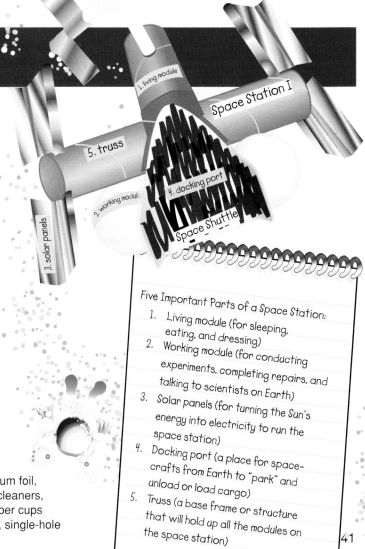

1. living module

Space Station I

5. truss

2. working module

4. docking port

3. solar panels

Space Shuttle

Five Important Parts of a Space Station:
1. Living module (for sleeping, eating, and dressing)
2. Working module (for conducting experiments, completing repairs, and talking to scientists on Earth)
3. Solar panels (for turning the Sun's energy into electricity to run the space station)
4. Docking port (a place for spacecrafts from Earth to "park" and unload or load cargo)
5. Truss (a base frame or structure that will hold up all the modules on the space station)

Suggested materials: paper towel and toilet paper tubes, aluminum foil, bendable drinking straws, small Styrofoam® deli trays, yarn, pipe cleaners, wooden or plastic spools, Styrofoam craft balls, different-sized paper cups and plastic containers, construction paper, newspaper, cardboard, single-hole puncher, scissors, tape, markers and crayons

3, 2, 1...Blast Off!
(Demonstration)

Materials: 2 long party balloons lightly dusted with cornstarch; nylon monofilament fishing line; 2 plastic drinking straws; 1 Styrofoam® cup; 2 binder clips; masking tape; regular tape; scissors

Use the following demonstration to show your students how the space shuttle and other space-craft use multistage rockets to blast into space. Begin by explaining that a *multistage rocket* consists of two or more rockets that are stacked on top of each other or side by side. Further explain that the rockets use up their energy (fuel) one at a time, then drop off so the remaining rockets have less weight to carry as they climb toward space. Collect the materials shown and follow the directions to demonstrate how multistage rockets work. Recruit another teacher or a parent volunteer to assist.

Directions:
1. Thread the fishing line through both straws. Stretch the line taut across a room and use masking tape to tape each end to a wall.
2. Cut the top off the Styrofoam cup, creating an open-ended ring.
3. Stretch out both balloons; then inflate one balloon about three-quarters full. Twist the nozzle and attach a binder clip to it to keep the air in. Slide the nozzle end through the ring, as shown.
4. Partially inflate the second balloon and slide the front of it through the ring; then fully inflate it. Attach a binder clip as shown.
5. Use regular tape to tape both balloons to the straws on the fishing line. Slide the balloons to the end of the fishing line so that the nozzles are facing the closest wall.
6. Remove the binder clip from the first balloon and pinch the end closed. Then, together with students, begin a countdown for a rocket blastoff. Remove the binder clip from the second balloon and let the balloons go. *(The second balloon will release all of its air. Then the first balloon will release its air and finish the trip along the fishing line.)*

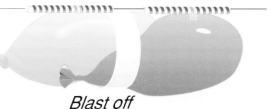

Blast off

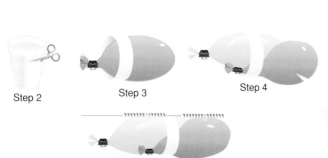

Step 2   Step 3   Step 4

Step 4

Super Space Shuttle
(Making a Model)

What blasts off like a rocket, has wings like a plane, orbits like a satellite, and lands like a glider? The space shuttle, of course! Use the following activity to give your students a cross-section view of this hardworking vehicle. First, explain that NASA developed the reusable shuttle to make space travel less expensive. Further explain that the shuttle is made up of four parts—two rocket boosters, an external fuel tank, and the orbiter. The two *rocket boosters* and the engines on the orbiter boost the shuttle into space. The rocket boosters drop off the shuttle after two minutes. The external fuel tank uses up its fuel, then drops off the shuttle after 8½ minutes. The *orbiter* is the only part of the space shuttle that actually goes into space. Up to seven crew members can live and work in the *crew compartment*. There is also a *space lab,* a *cargo bay* where supplies and satellites are stored, and *three engines* that move the orbiter around in space. Have each student make her own model of the space shuttle similar to the one shown. Ahead of time cut out a class supply of 11½" x 3½" external fuel tanks from orange paper and two 10½" x 1" rocket boosters from white construction paper as shown. Then provide each child with the materials listed and guide her through the directions. Encourage each student to take her space shuttle home to share with her family.

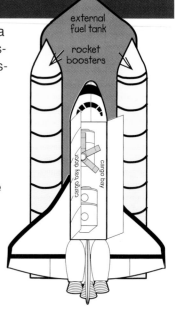

external fuel tank

rocket boosters

cargo bay door

cargo bay door

cargo bay

Materials: 1 external fuel tank cutout, 2 rocket booster cutouts, 1 white construction paper copy of page 46, scissors, glue, markers or crayons

Directions:
1. Glue the rocket booster cutouts onto each side of the external fuel tank cutout as shown.
2. Cut out the shuttle pattern (A).
3. Cut out patterns B and C. Fold each tab back along the dotted lines.
4. Place a dot of glue behind each tab; then attach B and C to the back of A as shown, creating two doors over the shuttle's flight deck and crew quarters.
5. Cut out pattern D. Place a bead of glue where indicated; then attach D to A as shown. Fold along the dotted lines, creating two flaps (cargo bay doors). (See illustration on page 46.)
6. Cut out pattern E. Place a bead of glue along the back of the pattern. Then glue E on top of D as shown.
7. Place a bead of glue along the back of the shuttle orbiter; then attach the orbiter to the external fuel tank as shown.

Astronaut Training Minicamp
(Simulation Training Activities)

Let your students find out if they have the right stuff to be astronauts by completing Astronaut Training Minicamp. Enlist the help of parent volunteers to man the stations. Divide your class into four groups to rotate through the stations. Duplicate page 47 for each student to fill out upon completion of each station.

Training Mission 1: Get Fit for the Trip

Explain to students that astronauts must be physically fit. Have each student complete the fitness activities shown. Adjust the rate of exercise and allow for rest periods as needed. Be sure students stretch before beginning and cool down afterward.

1. **Jumping Jacks**—Do ten, rest for 15 seconds, and then do ten more.
2. **Running**—Run in place for three minutes.

Training Mission 2: Space Snacks

Most astronaut food is dehydrated, freeze-dried, preserved by its packaging, or nonperishable. Astronauts add water to many foods and heat them before eating. Have students prepare their own space snacks. Ahead of time request from a local fast-food restaurant a class set of paper beverage cups with lids and straw holes. Then purchase instant drink mix, aluminum foil, straws, and snack items such as peanuts, pretzels, dry cereal, and raisins. Pour the snack items into bowls. Provide each student with a length of aluminum foil, a beverage cup, a lid, and a straw. Allow each student to spoon snacks onto his aluminum foil square. Then help the student fold the foil into a packet. Next, have the student place several spoonfuls of instant drink mix into his cup. Direct the student to place his lid on the cup. Have each student carefully fill his cup with water through the straw hole on the lid, insert his straw, and stir before enjoying his beverage and eating his space snack.

Training Mission 3: Suit Up for Space

Explain to students that because there is no atmosphere in space, astronauts must take their own atmospheres, in the form of space suits, with them on space walks. Further explain that most space suits allow astronauts to move and work while protecting them from heat, radiation, and small flying debris. Space suits are airtight, pressurized, and temperature and humidity controlled. Have each student design her own space suit by providing her with a length of bulletin board paper (five to six feet long) and markers or crayons. Display an enlarged copy of the space suit diagram shown. Have students work in pairs to trace each other's body outline onto the bulletin board paper. Next, have each student use the space suit diagram to help her draw and label a simple space suit on her body outline. Display these space suits in the hallway where all of your astronauts-in-training can view them.

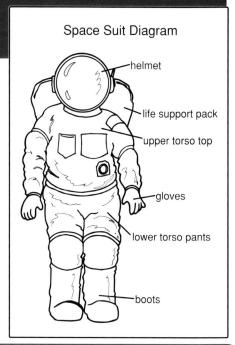

Space Suit Diagram

- helmet
- life support pack
- upper torso top
- gloves
- lower torso pants
- boots

Training Mission 4: Astronaut Activities

Explain to students that NASA chooses about 20 astronaut candidates every two years. These candidates must be fast learners, healthy, and able to handle stress and work well with others. Once in space, shuttle astronauts perform many different jobs. Discuss the astronaut careers shown with your students; then have each child decide which job she would like best. Next, have each student write a letter to NASA explaining why she would be a perfect candidate for a career in space. Send the letters to NASA Code FE, 300 East Street SW, Washington, DC 20546.

Spacecraft Jobs:

Pilots command and fly the spacecraft. Most pilot astronauts are military test pilots. *Mission specialists* maintain the spacecraft, conduct experiments, perform space walks, and launch satellites. *Payload specialists* also conduct experiments, usually for the owner of the spacecraft's cargo. They are approved by NASA.

43

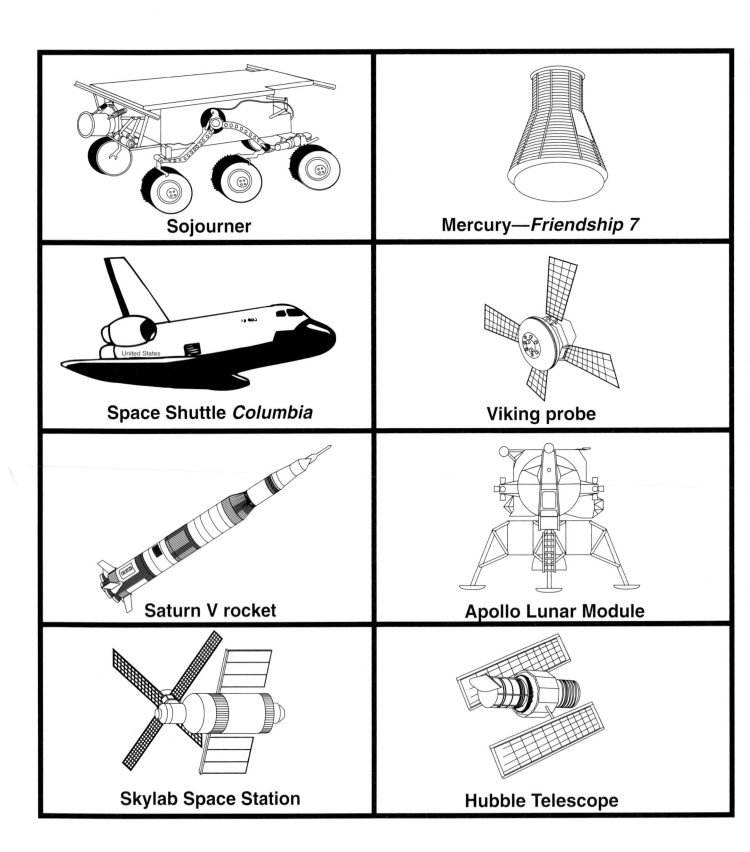

Sojourner

Mercury—*Friendship 7*

Space Shuttle *Columbia*

Viking probe

Saturn V rocket

Apollo Lunar Module

Skylab Space Station

Hubble Telescope

Note to the teacher: Use with "What's Been Up There?" on page 40.

Two **Viking probes** were sent to Mars. These probes didn't carry astronauts, but they did carry computers.

Date: 1975

Skylab was the first space station launched from the United States. Humans could live and work on this space station.

Date: 1973

A satellite called the **Hubble Telescope** was launched from a space shuttle. This satellite orbits (goes around Earth) collecting data for scientists back on Earth.

Date: 1990

The **Apollo Lunar Module** was used to land astronauts Buzz Aldrin and Neil Armstrong on the Moon. Neil Armstrong became the first person to step on the surface of the Moon.

Date: 1969

The first American astronaut launched into space was John Glenn. He *orbited,* or flew around, Earth three times in a **Mercury** spacecraft called *Friendship 7.*

Date: 1962

The **space shuttle** is the first spacecraft that can be used again and again. Two rocket boosters lift the shuttle into space. Seven astronauts can live and work in the shuttle for about 30 days.

Date: 1981

Sojourner was the first small robotlike car, or rover, to land on Mars. It was used to study rocks on the planet and help scientists learn that there once was water on Mars.

Date: 1997

For many years the **Saturn V** rockets were used to send the *Apollo* spacecrafts into space. These launching rockets were the largest and most powerful ever built.

Date: 1968

©2000 The Education Center, Inc. • *Investigating Science* • Solar System • TEC1745

Note to the teacher: Use with "What's Been Up There?" on page 40.

45

Patterns

Use with "Super Space Shuttle" on page 42.

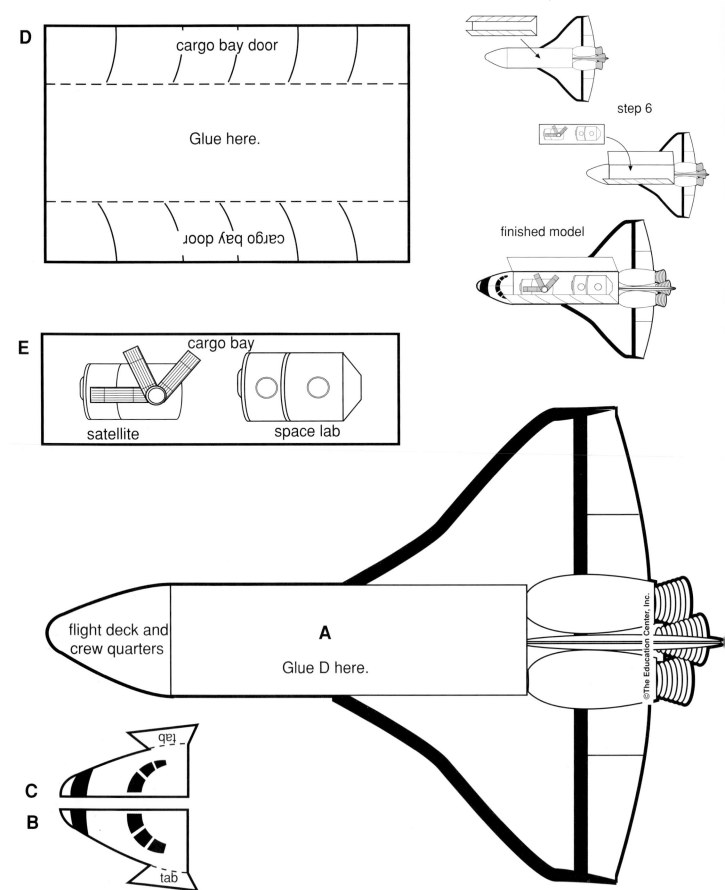

D

cargo bay door

Glue here.

cargo bay door

step 5

step 6

finished model

E

cargo bay

satellite

space lab

flight deck and
crew quarters

A

Glue D here.

©The Education Center, Inc.

C

B

tab

tab

Astronaut
Training Experience Log

Name: _____

I think astronauts should be physically fit because _____
_____
_____.

I would like/dislike eating astronaut food because _____
_____
_____.

The astronaut job I would like best would be _____
because _____
_____.

An astronaut's space suit is important because _____
_____
_____.

©2000 The Education Center, Inc. • *Investigating Science* • *Solar System* • TEC1745

Note to the teacher: Use with "Astronaut Training Minicamp" on page 43.

Answer Keys

Page 7

Landscape
Venus—Dry and rocky; lots of volcanoes
Earth—Contains deserts, forests, oceans, mountains, etc.

Surface Temperature
Venus—Up to 915°F
Earth— –94° to 131°F

Atmosphere
Venus—Poisonous (carbon dioxide and traces of nitrogen)
Earth—Air (not poisonous); made up of nitrogen, oxygen, and water vapor

Rotation Direction
Venus—East to west
Earth—West to east

Size (Diameter)
Venus—7,521 miles (12,104 km)
Earth—7,926 miles (12,756 km)

Distance From Sun
Venus—67,000,000 miles (108,000,000 km)
Earth—93,000,000 miles (150,000,000 km)

Page 9

Mercury
Distance from the Sun = 36 million miles (58 million km)
Number of moons = 0
Order of planet from the Sun = 1st
1 year on Mercury = 88 Earth days
1 day on Mercury = 58 days, 14 hours on Earth

Venus
Distance from the Sun = 67 million miles (108 million km)
Number of moons = 0
Order of planet from the Sun = 2nd
1 year on Venus = 224.7 Earth days
1 day on Venus = 243 days, 5 hours on Earth

Earth
Distance from the Sun = 93 million miles (150 million km)
Number of moons = 1
Order of planet from the Sun = 3rd
1 year on Earth = 365.2 Earth days
1 day on Earth = 23 hours, 56 minutes on Earth

Page 10

Mars
Distance from the Sun = 142 million miles (228 million km)
Number of moons = 2
Order of planet from the Sun = 4th
1 year on Mars = 687 Earth days
1 day on Mars = 24 hours, 37 minutes on Earth

Jupiter
Distance from the Sun = 438 million miles (778 million km)
Number of moons = 16
Order of planet from the Sun = 5th
1 year on Jupiter = 11.9 Earth years
1 day on Jupiter = 9 hours, 50 minutes on Earth

Saturn
Distance from the Sun = 886 million miles (1,427 million km)
Number of moons = 18
Order of planet from the Sun = 6th
1 year on Saturn = 29.5 Earth years
1 day on Saturn = 10 hours, 14 minutes on Earth

Page 11

Uranus
Distance from the Sun = 2 billion miles (3 billion km)
Number of moons = 17
Order of planet from the Sun = 7th
1 year on Uranus = 84 Earth years
1 day on Uranus = 17 hours, 14 minutes on Earth

Neptune
Distance from the Sun = 3 billion miles (4 billion km)
Number of moons = 8
Order of planet from the Sun = 8th
1 year on Neptune = 164.8 Earth years
1 day on Neptune = 16 hours, 7 minutes on Earth

Pluto
Distance from the Sun = 3.5 billion miles (6 billion km)
Number of moons = 1
Order of planet from the Sun = 9th
1 year on Pluto = 247.7 Earth years
1 day on Pluto = 6 days, 9 hours on Earth